# THE ELD

Doreen Fletcher was born an awfully long time ago, and has been writing verses for as long as anyone can remember. Several of her rhymes have been published in anthologies and magazines over the years. At the age of 62 Doreen passed her driving test (although she's never been able to afford a car) and at the age of 72 she graduated from the Open University with a BA. She sings in one choir, two madrigal groups and makes rather splendid cakes and lemon curd.

Doreen lives with her piano and word-processor in Farnham, Surrey, in the house where she was born. She has two middle-aged children, two grandchildren, and a beautiful park at the bottom of her garden.

# THE
# ELDERLY SAGE

*Ageing Rhymes from an
Ageing Lady*

*by*
DOREEN FLETCHER

*Illustrations by
Heather Colman*

A GAUDIN BENET BOOK

the PARSNIP BUTTERY

First published in 1995 by
The Parsnip Buttery
13 Holyrood Road, Northampton NN5 7AH
01604 585428

© Doreen Fletcher, 1995

All rights reserved. No part of this
publication may be reproduced in any form
or by any means – graphic, electronic, or
mechanical, including photocopying,
recording, taping or information storage
and retrieval systems – without the prior
permission in writing of the publishers.

British Library Cataloguing in Publication
Data. A catalogue record for this book is
available from the British Library

ISBN 0 9526519 0 4

Cover design and typesetting by
Heather Colman
Printed by The Guildhall Press, Northampton

## PREFACE

I hope
   – to make this book worth while –
That you will say
   "How true!"
      and smile.

## Contents

| | |
|---|---|
| The Elderly Sage | 11 |
| Window Shopping | 12 |
| The Ferryman | 13 |
| The Omission | 14 |
| That Waiting Room | 15 |
| Lost for Words | 16 |
| Coming for a Song | 17 |
| The Shoelace | 17 |
| Conservation | 18 |
| Relativity | 19 |
| Discourse | 19 |
| Follow That | 20 |
| Back to Basics | 20 |
| Casting a Blind Eye | 21 |
| The Case | 22 |
| The Supermarket War | 23 |
| The Missing Link | 24 |
| The Optimist | 26 |
| Bothering about Benches | 26 |
| High Living | 27 |
| Nostalgia | 28 |
| Decimalisation | 28 |
| Ask a Policeman | 29 |

# Contents

| | |
|---|---|
| The Look-alike | 30 |
| Winter | 31 |
| The Hoarder | 32 |
| The Weave | 33 |
| Walking Home | 34 |
| The Long Tin Bath | 35 |
| Bringing Back the Basics | 36 |
| Degeneration | 38 |
| Bother! | 38 |
| Looking Back | 39 |
| Shopping | 40 |
| The Diary | 41 |
| Short-Term Fuse | 42 |
| The Visitor's Lament | 42 |
| The Fallacy | 43 |
| Safe Custody | 43 |
| Furring | 44 |
| A Descending Scale | 45 |
| Keeping Fit | 46 |
| Making up for Lost Time | 46 |
| I Before E | 47 |
| Elasticity | 47 |
| The Chore | 48 |

## Contents

- The Slur ............ 49
- Down Below ............ 49
- Matchless Misery ............ 50
- Disorientation at Oxford Circus ............ 51
- Expendability ............ 52
- Great Aunt Fan ............ 52
- The Mission ............ 53
- Freedom to Roam ............ 54
- *Fine* ............ 55
- Reminiscing ............ 55
- Tea Time ............ 56
- My Supermarket Friend ............ 56
- To Get Ahead ............ 57
- The Pedant ............ 58
- Gears ............ 59
- Extortion ............ 59
- Dialogue ............ 60
- Charterhouse Summer School of Music ............ 61
- The List ............ 62
- The Unwelcome Guest ............ 62
- Making Sure ............ 63

## Contents

Footprints in the Sand ............ 64
The Garden ................................. 65
Keeping Up .................................. 65
The Half-Remembered Spring ... 66
Apple Blossom ........................... 67
Black Lead .................................. 68
The Wireless .............................. 68
Lethargy ..................................... 69
The Self-Locking System ........... 70
A Subject for Conversation ..... 71
The Pre-Farr Era ....................... 72

# The Elderly Sage

Alas, with mounting years I find
   that folk are apt to doubt
When I hold forth on matters I know
   I know all about,
And then there are occasions when the
   law I'm laying down,
My listeners raise an eyebrow
   or, alternatively, frown.

Quite recently, I said out loud that
   everybody knew
Lord Nelson, gallant seaman, met his
   end at Waterloo;
That Harold, king of great repute, was
   gravely in a fix
At Hastings, in a battle fought in 1366.

I also told my Uncle Albert
   (sadly now quite dead)
The live wire for a plug is blue...
   though previously red;
And on the subject of the humps
   beneath the desert sun,
The dromedary has the two,
   the Bactrian just the one.

Maybe my erudition is thought suspect by a few,
Still, everyone might be prepared to give to me my due.
Although old age has moved me to the wings from centre stage,
Do not my years befit me for my newfound role of "sage"?

## Window Shopping

I love to go to town upon a window-shopping spree,
A leisurely perambulation for an hour or three,
And, as I never buy a thing, the only cash I blue
Is what I spend (this once was just a penny) on the loo!

## The Ferryman

I wonder if the Ferryman's a merry man –
If he smiles as he manipulates the oars.
I wonder if he sings to cheer his passengers
And if they recompense him with applause.

I wonder if he takes his clients singly,
Or if he rows a boatload at a time.
I wonder if he asks for any payment,
Or takes the view that this would be a crime.

I wonder if he's lonely when he's rowing back,
Or if he's glad to have the extra space.
I wonder if he takes his time returning,
Or just treats every journey as a race.

I wonder if, when summoned by appointment,
He'll let a disapproving frown appear.
I wonder, if the traveller is youthful,
His heart is touched – he's moved to shed a tear.

I'm quite aware that one day I shall
  meet him
And he can tell me what I wish to know,
But until then I'm happy to keep
  wond'ring –
For, frankly, I am in no rush to go.


## THE OMISSION

Dolly Stanton learned her Latin verbs
  in Class 4b
Along with Mary Hughes,
  Renata Merriman and me.
I know that there were others,
  but unhappily I find
I may recall their faces, but their
  names have slipped my mind.

I have a rolled-up photograph to which
  I can refer,
A record of the complement in 1934.
But all it gives is *faces* and I've just
  myself to blame:
I should have made an allied chart
  ascribing every name.

But I didn't!

## That Waiting Room

There was a time when I might pay a
 visit once a year,
But with my little disc I was at least
 afforded cheer
In that I had some measure of how long
 I had to wait,
Subtracting from my number what the
 indicator'd state.

My visits now have multiplied,
 the discs are thrown away.
Instead the "timed appointments" are
 the order of the day.
But with this innovation both the
 nurses and the docs
Decided on a spring-clean and disposed
 of all their clocks.

With frequencies of visits and the
 endless time I've spent,
I could well be presented with a bill
 made out for rent
So, why not take my duvet and,
 migrating down the road,
Move in and make that waiting room
 my permanent abode?

## Lost for Words

These tiny cupboards in my mind,
To which I've lost the key,
Are crammed with words I cannot find
And cause me misery.

The nouns, they say, are first to go –
The names of things and persons –
While verbs, those action words, are slow
In making their desertions.

But as my missing words I chase
I doubt this supposition,
For I'm as likely to misplace
The simplest preposition!

These tiny cupboards in my mind
To which I've lost the key,
Are crammed with words I cannot find
And cause me misery.

The answer I have found today –
For you will shortly see me
Lock *every* English word away
And learn to speak Swahili!

## Coming for a Song

My wardrobe has labels of which I am
  proud
So I wear all my clothes with aplomb.
There's nothing that's brash and there's
  nothing that's loud,
With Jean Muir I can never go wrong!

I've even a Hartnell, a Dior or two,
And the reason? I've made the selection
Of all of my clothes
  (not a one is brand new)
From the
  Oxfam Haute Couture Collection.


## The Shoelace

My feet from my fingers
In yardage
Measures surely the same
As when I was twenty-two,
So why the gap
So hard to bridge
When now I try
To tie my shoe?

## Conservation

A green, a church, a pub with thatch,
Some rose-rimmed cottage doors.
A miniature emporium –
The village general stores.

A friendly bobby on the beat,
A milkman on his rounds –
An anvil ringing in the forge
And church bells – happy sounds.

The green is now a hyperstore,
The church turned into flats,
The bobby in a Panda car
Divorced from friendly chats.

The forge has vanished – milkman gone,
Small dwellings once so prized
Have disappeared, gone without trace –
The village urbanised.

Your knowledge is of former days?
Preserve it from attack
And keep the village as it was
By never going back.

## Relativity

"You're growing old",
   they say with piteous look
And I agree – no getting off the hook.
But can't they see, I'm not the only one –
The process starts the moment
   life's begun.

"You're growing old",
   they say, and with this cue
I gently tell them,
   "Yes, but so are you!
The difference is –
   though *you* may be the stronger,
*I've* played at growing old
   that little longer!"

## Discourse

I hold such interesting conversations
Which entertain and please exceedingly.
No wonder, as these verbal delectations
Are dialogues between myself and me!

## Follow That

My mother gave me fish and chips
    and treacled spotted dick,
And on my bread (this white) was
    often dripping dripping thick.
With sugar by the ton so many things
    she used to bake
Like scrumptious jam-filled doughnuts
    and delicious lardy cake.
I'd richest milk straight from the churn
    with cream on special days
And savouries upon the plate had salt
    thrown in a haze.
I wonder now, how is it I have managed
    to survive,
For by today's decrees I have
    no right to be alive!

## Back to Basics

The Flatiron and the Acme
Were once my household friends,
And now it's hard to come to terms
With all the modern trends.

The gadgets, their instructions,
Have me totally confused,
That video I had installed...
It still remains unused.

Machines that wash the clothes and pots
Eclipse the kitchen sink,
But who can give a guarantee
They won't go on the blink?

And when these "treasures" do break down –
Such happenings increase –
I'm tempted to inter the lot
And exhume elbow grease!

## Casting a Blind Eye

Household chores have never been
  my favourite pursuit.
In spite of this my diligence has not
  been in dispute.
But oh, what joy, since getting older
  I'm no longer fussed –
For with my failing eyesight I'm not
  conscious of the dust.

## The Case

When I was young the pedant said,
   "The word is 'I' not 'me',
Ignoring this you'll find no way
   to climb the social tree."
So many folk have reached the top
   by heeding this advice
But now will throw an "I" in any time
   – not thinking twice.

The greatest danger lies where
   prepositions rear their head,
With that conjunction "and" to make
   the meaning further spread.
And so, upon the radio, the
   television too,
You'll hear presenters, politicians –
   naming but a few –

With devastating confidence proceed
   to fall from grace,
Disseminating "I"s where clearly
   "me"s have right of place.
They fail to think about the case
   applying to the word,
Just ploughing on regardless of the fact
   they might have erred.

Pedants come and pedants go –
   a language moves along –
But still there's room to comment
   if it's thought the use is wrong.
And if you're one of those who err,
   no matter how you try,
I pray that you will profit from this
   homily...and...I?

## THE SUPERMARKET WAR

There's Somerfield (that's Gateway)
   versus Sainsbury and the like,
With Tesco fighting Safeway,
   even Kwik Save and St Mike.
It's cut-throat competition
   that is seen to grow apace
In the limited confinement
   of the supermarket space.
Where is this mighty battlefield?
Where is this weighty war?
Among the thousand plastic bags
   I've stuffed tight in a drawer!

## The Missing Link

I'd better stop and listen as it's near
   five minutes to,
For if I don't I won't hear what the
   weather's going to do.
I need to know in order I may organise
   my day,
Ensuring that it's planned in the most
   advantageous way.

There's washing waiting to be done
   involving hanging out;
The garden may need water if there's
   little rain about;
And there's the Fete this afternoon
   that's on from twelve to four –
I'd like to go, but not if all it's going to
   do is pour.

Oh, good! It's Michael Fish this
   morning – such a friendly voice –
Of all the weather forecasters he'll
   always be my choice.
He's starting with the top of Britain,
   making his way down.
Scotland's weather's not so good –
   that's bound to cause a frown.

Some scattered showers about The Wash
   and thunderstorms in Gwent.
Now *there's* a place I know quite well
   – the many weeks I've spent
On holiday in Wales – those memories
   come flooding back,
Such happy times with Mum and Dad,
   Aunt Flo and Uncle Jack.

There was the time Aunt Flo transgressed
   and fell foul of the law,
And we all fell about with laughing
   loudly when we saw
That all that she had done was take the
   bit between her teeth
And race about at midnight in the
   streets of Pontypridd.

Of course, with due admonishing they
   had to let her go
And we all celebrated down a local
   pub…
     But, oh,
He's on to "outlook" now –
   I might have known –
     it's very clear
The bit I *should* have listened to I
   simply didn't hear!

## The Optimist

In vain have I tried to throw out
   that old pail.
I know there's a hole,
   'cos it left a wet trail.
I accept that it seems
   to have no use today,
But who is to tell?
   By tomorrow
      it may.

## Bothering about Benches

Was I ever bothered about benches?
Did I ever sigh to find a seat –
Find myself when on my constitutional,
Plagued by aching legs or weary feet?

Would I, at a party, make a beeline
To anything remotely like a chair,
Convinced that if deprived of such
   a comfort
I'd founder floorwards, causing folk
   to stare.

My memory won't tell me what the
 truth is –
I'm not sure that I'm able to avow
That sitting *was* of paramount
 importance
But, oh my goodness, it's of moment
 now!

## High Living

I sit and watch my television
 programmes every night,
But sometimes crave a change –
 a different menu of delight.
To visiting the cinema I would not
 be averse,
The problem is the price – now so
 much larger than my purse.
Today it's pounds I have to pay for
 just a single seat
And I'd need two – some company
 to make the jaunt complete.
So still I sit and watch TV,
 but how my spirit pines
For all those hours of luxury
 found in the one-and-nines*. \*9p

## Nostalgia

I carry in my head "As Time Goes By"
And think of "Stormy Weather"
   with a sigh.
Nostalgia – there is more than just a twinge
In longing for the days of Fred and Ginge.
Today's fare is, alas, not up my street –
It's mostly loud cacophony and beat;
And so, what joy I feel when someone
   plays
The pleasing diet of my Salad Days.


## Decimalisation

I grew up with the ten-bob note,
  the pound,
    the pint,
      the yard,
And so it is quite natural
  I find conversion hard.
I've come to terms with 50ps
  and even with the metre,
But still cannot accommodate
  the kilo and the litre.

By counting years in decimals,
   I'm nearer eight than seven
And doubt that there'll be measuring
   of anything in heaven.
It seems a waste of time to learn
   to change one to the other
And, thinking of the strain involved,
   I don't intend to bother.

## Ask a Policeman

If I needed to know the time of the day,
Or if ever I was not quite sure of the way,
Help was at hand – a uniformed force
Patrolled all the streets as a matter
   of course.

It's thought that policemen to one
   growing old
Look younger and younger (at least,
   so I'm told).
To check that it's true I have searched
   high and low,
But they've all disappeared – I can't
   prove that it's so.

## The Look-Alike

I have stayed on this side of my face now
For seventy years and some more.
The jibe that it's aged –
　"a disgrace!" now –
An arraignment I'm bound to deplore.

I'm seventeen years here inside, so
My youth must reflect in what's seen.
No wonder this view I deride so –
That my image is grey and not green.

Alas, the mirage could not last me;
It vanished like fast-melting snow
Through a visitor out of the past – she
A school friend from long, long ago.

The oldest of ladies who stood there,
As I opened the door to my chum,
Said, "I've come to see Doreen
　who lives here,
I take it that you are her Mum."

## Winter

The ice age is upon me just as soon as
  winter comes.
I'm colder as I'm older and deplore the
  way it numbs
    My hands and feet and often
      sends my circulation spare.
I wish I lived in torrid tropic climes
  – I don't –
    but there,
I'm often told,
  "Of circumstances
    one should make the best",
So, "Bless my mittens, bed socks and
  – what's more –
    my thermal vest!"

## The Hoarder

I counted the plastic containers
Retained when the contents were done,
And remembered my drastic disclaimers
If accused as a hoarder by some.
I threw out a quarter
  (that meant thirty-three)
And was self-satisfied for a while,
But that feeling soon faded,
I just retrograded
And found I had doubled the pile.

Once more I threw out just a quarter,
Thus fifty containers were dead.
The rest felt distrust for this slaughter –
They multiplied threefold instead.
I thought to myself,
  "Now this simply won't do!
For such conduct I have no excuse,
There is only one thing
A solution will bring –
From now on, I buy *only* what's loose."

## The Weave

I find it so hard to conceive
How my walk's been transformed to
 a "weave".
I'm sure once I was fine,
Made my way in a line,
At least that's what I'd like to believe.

I don't think that it can be endearing
This bothersome penchant for veering –
It is hard to endure
And I long for a cure
To repair my malfunctioning steering.

It's no help, each appendage below
Has decided to strike or go slow.
Though my sense of direction
Needs constant correction,
My lower limbs don't want to know.

I'm inclined to surrender to gloom
At my treating each path as a loom,
But why should I fret
If I'm happy to bet
I can still weave my wavy way home?

## Walking Home

I still remember when
Most shops were open until ten
And in the dark folk went on foot
   to meet
      And gossip in the street.
Today, when coming home by night
From some place where I've been
   to celebrate,
There is an emptiness about the town
Which makes me conscious I'm alone.
There are occasions when I look
   behind
      To prove it's only shadows that
         I'll find –
A stupid thing, I'm told, to fret upon,
It's young men (not the old)
Who are most likely to be set upon.

PS:
Perhaps, but I am certain that
   safety would obtain
If streets at night were peopled by
   the people once again.

## The Long Tin Bath

I have a childhood memory
Of which I'll never tire –
It's lounging in a long tin bath
Before a roasting fire.

Essential to ensure
That you don't touch the hottest side,
An omnipresent peril
As you stand up to be dried.

Now it's porcelain or plastic,
And no fire lit in the hearth,
I pity all those younger folk
Who've missed the long tin bath.

## Bringing Back the Basics

I'm all for bringing back the quill
    and abacus,
In doing so, restore the simple life.
Re-activating them cannot be bad for us
But do a lot of good where stress is rife.

I'm sure, to use the simple frame and
    feather
Would prove to be the source of much
    delight.
Unhappy souls found straining at their
    tether
Might smile again and see their future
    bright.

How often with my trolley I stand by
    a till,
While anxious staff attempt to trace
    the fault,
And twenty folk behind me too have
    had their fill
Of highest tech machines not worth
    their salt.

I murmur to the nearest shopper,
  "Rods with beads
Should really be the order of the day –
Would satisfy much better their
  accounting needs.
I've told them, but they scoff at what I say."

And then, returning home some three
  hours later,
I settle down to word-process an ode.
What do I find? The Amstrad's ceased
  to cater
For what I want, – in fact, it might
  explode.

I press a hundred keys in sheer
  frustration,
Still, messages (quite rude) invade the
  screen,
And so, as I review the situation,
I dream of quills and sigh for what
  has been.

I'm all for bringing back the quill and
  abacus
But then, on second thoughts, I feel
  dismay.
In calling for a world that is computerless,
I ask myself, "What would the
  *children* say?"

## Degeneration

Not quite an Audrey Hepburn, nor yet
   Diana Dors,
My figure, in its prime, still drew –
   OK, polite – applause.
With time, there's no disputing it, some
   flattening's occurred,
Those ins and outs which **once** were mine
Are now quite simply blurred!


## Bother!

I often wonder, when I've overheard
The utterance of some four-letter word,
Just why it is that time has seemed to play
"Manipulating words" (consider, "gay").

But then I think, what does it signify?
Or, come to that, where does the
   problem lie?
*True* meaning's found – and nothing
   can be clearer –
Entirely in the ear of the behearer.

## Looking Back

My measure stretches longer as I live.
From childhood, growing old,
   I've felt it give.
Until today I find to my surprise
How close the past historically lies.
From birth a striding just three times
   my span
Would take me to Her Majesty
   Queen Anne.
And, if I chose, with four I'd come upon
A Cromwell (Ollie) or a Milton (John).
And then one step beyond –
   from four to five
I'd reach the time when Shakespeare
   was alive.

"What brought this on?", you say.
To tell you I've no qualms
I realised my Mother shared
Ten years or more with Brahms!

## Shopping

I shop, I reach the checkout till
And now I have to pay,
And each time I resolve that
I shall not cause a delay,

The checkout girl works with
  such speed
She's done before I'm packed
(But then, she has no option for,
If slow, she might be sacked).

I fumble as I stow the goods –
Feel things could not get worse.
How wrong I am, all goes downhill
When I unzip my purse.

The pennies slither, notes get stuck,
Pounds plummet to the floor.
I hear impatient sighs
As 10ps roll towards the door.

If only people understood –
My plight does have a reason,
It's this – the digits – I have reached
The fifty-finger season!

So – I must choose a "packing" till
With helper there to fix it
And, as for paying cash, it's clear
In future I must "Switch" it!

## The Diary

I asked a man to come and sweep
   the chimneys,
A helpful friend to come and perm
   my hair,
A cousin to escort me to the dentist,
A vicar to call round and say a prayer.

They all, as worthy folk,
   did as I asked them,
Arriving, they revealed a basic flaw –
I'd made no written record of
   arrangements
And so they met
   each other
      at my door.

## Short-Term Fuse

Just what was that witty remark
Which I made with such dashing
  aplomb?
Of its content I'm now in the dark
Though, when made, it went down like
  a bomb!

The sadness about my forgetting –
The reason it's brought me so low?
This gem causing so much upsetting
Was uttered three minutes ago!

## The Visitor's Lament

Oh, how one wishes
One were still allowed
To do the dishes
When one comes to stay!
But one is not wanted,
One has sadly been supplanted
By this *thing*
That washes dishes by machine!

## The Fallacy

And now, upon the matter that might vex,
That controversial subject – human sex.
The view that urge
  by age completely goes
Is wrong, and not included in our woes.

This leads me to deliver a corrective –
It's simply that we've got it in
  perspective.


## Safe Custody

I hid it in a special spot
For safety – so I thought.
I made the strongest mental note
For when it might be sought.

But, at the time for finding it,
The truth I had to face –
No matter where I searched, my prize
Had vanished without trace!

## Furring

In crisis or emergency I have to stop
   and think
Where once I knew just what to do
   before an eye could blink.
My repartee's retarded and my ripostes
   rarely heard.
My acumen in answering suggests my
   mind is furred.

And what does this add up to?
   I'm afraid that every year
Remorselessly my poor old brain
   slips into lower gear.
But by result my pace of life's
   relaxed into a stroll
And I can vouch, upon my heart,
   that I'm a happier soul.

Looking round about I see
   a mad right-royal rush
Of people hell for leather bent to jostle
   and to push.
To get from here to there within the
   minimum of time,
They'll willingly take risks that have
   no reason and no rhyme.

So bringing all this to account,
   I wonder if I'm right
In thinking there's a case to *stress* my
   state's not one of plight
And men and women, come what age,
   might find it fully fit
To follow my example –
   simply just slow down a bit.

## A Descending Scale

Singing in the choir has been my passion,
A high soprano voice has been my lot,
But recently I've seen it is the fashion
To move to alto as the voices drop.
I feel the time to change is coming on me
That shortly I shall have to face defeat.
But, no – I'll simply mime those wicked high notes
For, if I move, I'll lose my special seat.

## Keeping Fit

I have friends who aerobic,
    keep fit or Kung Fu,
Who avow their's the way
    constant youth to pursue.
The exercise *I've* found
    for this to be king –
Such a joyful pursuit –
    it is learning to *sing*.

## Making up for Lost Time

So many sights remain unseen,
Much music still unheard,
Such little time to do it in
Before I am interred.

All I can hope and trust is this
That when I do go over,
Conditions are that, nonetheless,
I'm still allowed to hover.

I before E

At school I won a book for spelling;
I was only ten.
Now I'm seven times that age
My spelling's down the drain.
No longer do I read that book
(One that was fictionary)
For – needs must – it's supplanted by
My English dictionary.


Elasticity

My circulation's slowed some more –
The doctor's cure is drastic –
"It's clear to me that you must wear
Some stockings of elastic!"

But still I feel quite put upon –
I just can't get the knack,
As what I need to pull them on
Is an elastic back!

## The Chore

It's a daily assignment, this
   troublesome chore,
A consumer of vigour and time.
I do it as I've always done it before,
Why I should has no reason or rhyme.

I know I'm exhausted and ready to cry
When I've come to a well-wanted end,
And that, if I wished,
   I could go out and buy
      A ready-made kit – it's the trend.

But the virtue of honest hard work
   would have flown
If I saw off the job in a twink.
And what's more, though I know that
   she's very long gone,
I can't *say* what my Mother would think!

## The Slur

How *can* you call it clutter,
   hand your heart on,
For all is neatly stored in box or
   carton,
In turn so neatly stacked from floor
   to ceiling –
I find such accusations
   *most* unfeeling.


## Down Below

Time was they all had platforms
Or stood six inches high,
And though I tottered quite a bit
Of course I had to try.
How glad I am that styles
   have changed
And My! How good it feels
To still be in the fashion
Wearing comfortable heels.

## Matchless Misery

I feel so alone – it's such trouble I'm in –
I am sure my complaint is unique.
My nose has turned green and has
    doubled in length
It grows longer, in fact, as I speak.

There are millions around who have
    just no idea
Of my misery, as I am sure
Such a dreadful condition as that
    which is mine
No one else has been asked to endure.

After hiding for months, I consult my GP
Who surveys me with gentle concern.
"So your nose has turned green and
    has doubled in length?
Not surprising! You may like to learn
You're the twentieth patient I've seen
    in a month
Who has suffered this unhappy fate.
You'll be well in a week if this potion
    you'll drink.
Your problem's just something you ate!"

## Disorientation at Oxford Circus

I came up from the Tube into the busy
 London crowd –
I looked around with puzzlement and
 nearly cried out loud –
No single corner shopfront did I
 recognise or know.
Surely when I came before was not
 *that* long ago?

I turned and checked the Station name,
 I found that it was right;
But hoards of unfamiliar signs
 elsewhere confirmed my plight.
I tried to get my bearings by returning
 down below
And coming up another side to see
 which way to go.

The people milled, the traffic roared,
 my head was in a spin,
Confusion reigned and no one cared
 the state that I was in.
At length, in desperation, I decided
 what to do,
I simply tossed the towel in and went
 back to Waterloo.

## Expendability

I learned how to darn
And I learned how to mend,
My shoes (when required)
To the cobblers I'd send.
"Conserving", "Preserving" –
The words of the day,
But now – no compunction –
Just throw it away!

## Great Aunt Fan

Our Great Auntie Fan had less face
   than had wrinkles;
Each "look-in" was purest delight.
When she laughed (as she *did*) then
   they all turned to crinkles.
Was ever a happier sight?

She would stand on the step of her
   tiny abode
Beaming her thanks for our visit.
No wonder that now, if my cares are
   a load,
This picture a smile will elicit.

## The Mission

I set out on a mission and I struggle
   up the stairs.
It's quite a feat for creaking limbs;
   at my age it compares
With running a full marathon
   or climbing Everest,
And so it's understandable
   that I should feel depressed

To find I've quite forgotten
   what I made the journey for.
I struggle to remember –
   even ask the bedroom door,
But I know from experience
   of workings of my brain
The only hope of recall is –
   go back and start again.

So this I do, returning to the bottom
   of the flight
Despairing – now there looms a *second*
   Everest in sight.
When shall I learn? I know quite well
   there is an antidote.
It's this – before I start out
   I must write myself a note!

## Freedom to Roam

My garden still extends out to some
  parkland,
To us in youth a joyous pleasure dome,
We children hastened off to play and
  lark and
Our Mums and Dads were happy
  staying home.

Now fear's intruded and the park's
  verboten
To young and old alone, and what
  is more
The Mums and Dads with children
  whom they dote on
Take care they never stray far from
  the door.

If those who pose a threat, when young,
  had wandered
Like us amid the butterflies and ferns,
Who knows? Potential joy might not
  be squandered
And happy days have many glad returns.

## FINE

I'm well upon my way now,
So relieved that I'm not knowing
Just what there is to come or
What the time is for my going.
But when my special song is sung –
My final ice-cream soda –
I hope that there will be for me
No elongated coda.


## REMINISCING

No one turns a hair if I should mention
  Valentino,
    Douglas Fairbanks,
      even "Putting on the Ritz",
But it's quite a different story –
From just "elderly", I'm "hoary"
If I dare to say,
  "Remember Zazu Pitts?"

## Tea Time

I'm partial to a pot of tea
At three or four pm.
This English custom you'll agree's
A first-class stratagem.

However, though I still do pour
The tea,  the custom sours,
As now I find that "three or four"
Is in the early hours!


## My Supermarket Friend

I never cared for banks
   (those mausoleums of the street)
And cash dispensers
   (these I know one day my card will eat)
So, welcome to my supermarket friend
   who, in a flash,
When I hand her my Switch card
   will replenish me with cash.

## To Get Ahead...

We all have our dreams
   and there's one that is mine –
An adornment to cheer as my life's
   in decline.
Not a tasteful tiara, or comely cravat,
But the bravest and bonniest
   broad-brimmèd hat.

It's a dream that I've carried along
   through the years
But it's still unfulfilled –
   just the thought brings me tears.
So, dressed up to the nines for some
   jaunt, nonetheless
I'm still plagued by sorrow –
   I'm "large titferless".

It's so long that I've thought of
   this charming chapeau
Be it chic or outrageous,
   avec or sans bow.
But what is the use
   now I'm seventy-plus?
I cannot deny it –
   I've quite missed the bus!

## The Pedant

I still conduct my conversation
   as when I was young
In language that is known to me,
   i.e. my Mother Tongue.
But years have passed and I cannot
   accept with any grace
The aggravating changes that with time
   have taken place.

There was an age, not long ago,
   when one would never try
To use the word "infer" when what
   was meant was to "imply".
New tricks of putting stresses where
   there may be some dispute –
A sample of this trait is in pronouncing
   *con*tribute.

But then I reassure myself –
   it's not so very strange
That things alive and kicking,
   such as language, suffer change.
And if I don't take care, this grievance
   I might overdo
Maintaining everyone should use
   a "thee" instead of "you".

## Gears

My trusty legs have served me well
Throughout my many years,
But now the strain's begun to tell –
I fear I've lost my gears.

There's one speed which I can attain,
It's one that's mighty slow.
Alas, it gives me such a pain
That faster I can't go.

But William Henry comes to mind –
Some compensation's there,
For, as I make my way I find
*More* "time to stand and stare".

## Extortion

When I've stumbled on streets that are cobbled,
When on pavements I've by-passed the cracks,
I say to myself, "I've been nobbled
By those who extort Council Tax!"

## Dialogue

Why should I always do just what
   I'm told?
Why should I take a back seat in
   the cold?
Why should I shrink from action
   that is bold?
*Because, my dear, you're old!*

Why can't I still in sunshine make
   some hay?
Why can't I to the bright lights make
   my way?
Why can't I join in youthful fun
   and play?
*Because you've had your day!*

Why should I dress in sepia or brown,
In sober colours make my way to town,
And never wear a puce or scarlet gown?
*Because your youth has flown!*

Why should I, hours and hours at
   home just sit,
With little else to do but read or knit?
Why can't I kick the traces just a bit?
*Because, my dear, it's fit!*

I listen to you, take in every word,
But know if I agreed then I'd have erred.
In fact your every comment is absurd!
*Concurred!*

## Charterhouse Summer School of Music

Some hundreds of yards from the school where we sing
Is the food and the beds where we slumber –
And therefore you'll see that my way I must wing
(This by foot) it seems times without number.

But finding the distance has suffered extension
This year, it is clear by a trick,
A rogue with a tractor and evil intention
Has moved the whole school brick by brick.

## The List

I had twenty-seven jobs yesterday.
Who would have thought it?
It's now today and, looking back,
I see that I've completed only two.
What happened to the other twenty-five?
They're still around,
  Vying with the further
    seventeen I've found.
My head is full and ready to explode.
I tell myself again,
  as competition grows
    (Although abortive order)
That I'd be wiser to resist
Determination *not* to make a list.

## The Unwelcome Guest

The muscle that I pulled
(How many months ago?)
Still hurts.
The ache –
When will it go away?
I suspect it's come to stay.

## Making Sure

Did I fasten the catch?
  Did I turn out the gas?
I'd better return just to see...
The catch has been fastened,
  the gas turned right off,
I'm relieved of my uncertainty.

I go off again – for some yards –
  then the thought –
Have I put out the bin for the men?
It's Tuesday,
  and I'm pretty certain I did...
But I'd better go back once again.

Reassured by its sight –
  there it is on the path –
I set out once more on my way.
Not for long, I'm afraid,
  for I come to a halt –
I am faced with another delay.

The catch, was it fastened?
  The gas, was it out?
I wonder..............

## Footprints in the Sand

What is there to show
To mark my being?
What left when I go
There for the seeing?

Tell me – where the worth
Affords my spending
Time upon the earth
There at my ending?

Words – a line or two
Arranged in order,
Not at all a cue
To say, "Applaud her!"

What of years remain
To fill the lacking?
Few, perhaps? It's plain
I must get cracking!

## The Garden

Spring comes –
Glad!
I find
Muscles and tendons
Forgotten I had.
Prognostication bad –
Weed-clad.
Sad!


## Keeping Up

I watch the younger generation
Following behind,
I'm fazed at times by new ideas
They seem to have in mind.
But – now is of the '90s
For my progeny *and* me.
So why should either one live
As in 1933?

## The Half-Remembered Spring

I'm so unhappy to announce
That somehow I've mislaid my bounce,
And as I plod along the street
With ten-ton weights upon my feet,
I long for those much happier days
When I was in receipt of praise
For my ability to skip
And even light fantastics trip.

Now, as I pump in oil of fish,
I turn around three times and wish
That this in time will help to bring
Return of half-remembered spring.
False hope, for it's not coming back
And so, to compensate the lack,
I've asked the State to intervene –
Lay on each path a trampoline.

Then, when I make my way to town,
No need to drag my feet or frown –
If they agree to do the job,
All that I'll need to do is BOB!

## Apple Blossom

My apple blossom days are gone,
The bloom has left my face;
Translucence that was youth has flown
With murk left in its place.

Yet autumn (with the apple trees)
May still a harvest bear –
A rounding that should likely ease
This strain of wear and tear.

And though my life may soon be gone
To leave a shrivelled fruit,
All is not lost – all hope not flown
In Nature's mad pursuit.

For springtimes come and come again
One's faith to underpin,
Through apple blossom that is plain
About a grandchild's skin.

## Black Lead

Black leading's a thing that belongs to
 the past,
But the pictures of grates and of ranges
And of kneelings to clean them,
 continue to last
After two generations of changes.

My thoughts of the kettle and pots
 on the boil
With the toast being made by the fire
Make me think, "Were we wise,
 though it was so much toil,
To let that black leading expire?"

## The Wireless

My father, many years ago,
 while at the table sat,
Spent hours and hours a-playing with
 the whiskers of a cat.
I wonder if he smiles to see,
 as he looks down from heaven,
That all I have to do today is
 simply press a button.

## Lethargy

That "get up and go" is retreating
More and more as the years roll along –
I've "let up", with no hope of beating
This comatose pull – it's so strong.

The vigour that once was, is fading,
I'm happy to sit in a chair –
The rigour of age all pervading –
So life's a lethargic affair.

Why don't I do something about it?
If I did, there's the risk I'd repent,
And I won't take the chance –
   if I flout it –
Of an epitaph, "Got Up And Went"!

# The Self-Locking System

The chair that has charms
   has a couple of arms
And a seat that's far-flung from the floor.
For with air all around,
   sitting nearer the ground,
There's a chance I'd be upright no more.

My joints have the gall,
   when they're angled at all,
To stay fixed as though fastened with glue,
So that prising them free
   from each other can be
An exercise painful to view.

Getting up from my chair
   had an elegant air
In the era described as "my prime".
But now when I rise
   this engagement requires
So much effort – what's more –
   so much *time*.

So what can I do? I can just say to you –
If you want me to move you had better
Leave nothing to chance,
   warn me well in advance
And confirm your requirements by letter.

## A Subject for Conversation

Common custom treating it
   a text at which to balk,
A topic that's unbroachable
   in seemly table talk,
A subject, if it's aired at all,
   that's classed among our fears,
Accompanied by downturned lips,
   by frowns, and even tears.

Enough of that – it's time to strike
   a much more merry tone,
And stress it's an adventure,
   although one we take alone.
Converse about it, chew it over,
   ventilate, discuss
As freely as we'd chat about
   a neighbour on a bus.

Then we life's single certainty
   may happily attend,
Our crossing of the border –
   a familiar friendly end.

THE PRE-FARR ERA
OR
TO MY JUNIOR
OR
A YEAR IN THE HAND...

---

I may be growing long of tooth,
My blood be rather thin,
Perchance my hair a gruesome grey
Above my double chin.

Maybe my hearing's rather hard,
My neck the scraggy sort,
My eyes no use without my specs,
My memory.....too short.

Another soul might argue –
As for me, I'll grant the lot
If you'll remember there were years
I WAS but you WERE NOT.